**Date Due**

|  |  |  |  |
|---|---|---|---|
|  |  |  |  |
|  |  |  |  |
|  |  |  |  |
|  |  |  |  |
|  |  |  |  |
|  |  |  |  |
|  |  |  |  |
|  |  |  |  |
|  |  |  |  |
|  |  |  |  |
|  |  |  |  |
|  |  |  |  |

# ALL THE PAINTINGS OF
## **CARAVAGGIO**
### *VOLUME SEVEN*
*in the*
*Complete Library of World Art*

*The Complete Library of World Art*

# ALL THE PAINTINGS

# OF **CARAVAGGIO**

*Edited by* COSTANTINO BARONI

*Translated by* ANTHONY FIRMIN O'SULLIVAN

HAWTHORN BOOKS, INC.

*Publishers · New York*

*Manufactured in Great Britain by Jarrold & Sons Ltd, Norwich*

# CONTENTS

# MICHELANGELO MERISI
# DA CARAVAGGIO

*Life and Work*

THE sixteen-year-old boy who knocked on the doors of Rome in search of lodgings shortly before 1590 had not left too many regrets behind him. Michelangelo Merisi was born at Caravaggio in Lombardy on September 28, 1573. His childhood was passed in the quiet atmosphere of that small town located between Brescia and Milan until, already orphaned about the age of eleven, he was sent to Milan to study painting. The four years at work there under Simone Peterzano must have seemed quite long to this restless boy, who was so eager for knowledge and so anxious to exceed what was permitted him by his master's mediocre Venetian-Lombard eclecticism. At that time great discoveries were being made in Milan, which was in the process of recovering from the terrible death toll brought by the plague of 1576. But the ascetic rigor of Archbishop Charles Borromeo on the one hand, and the commercial preoccupations of the Lombards on the other, were giving art a purely didactic purpose, so that the bold experiments of veristic painters like Antonio and Vicenzo Campi of Cremona, who were predecessors of Caravaggio, were almost unnoticed.

Under such circumstances the lure of Rome was most attractive to the more adventurous. Painters from Flanders and the Rhine continually passed through Milan. The vision summoning them was not so much that of the manneristic

Rome of Zuccari, Salviati, Muziano, and Fontana, and was even less the legendary Rome of the Golden Age of Raphael and Michelangelo. It was rather the city's aura of culture, the fascination of its ruins, the unrestrained effervescence of its artistic groups, and the enlightened patronage of the churchmen and patricians.

Lombards were pre-eminent at the Papal court as architects and sculptors, so that any artist might have felt at home in Rome, particularly one from Caravaggio. A few years earlier, a certain Giulio Merisi had distinguished himself as an architect there, along with his fellow-townsman Mangone. But this alone would hardly have enticed Caravaggio to Rome. Young Caravaggio had had quite enough of his family and his home town! His restive and mocking nature, as is revealed in the faun-like mask of the *Sick Bacchus* (plate 2) in the Borghese Gallery, led him into a risky and nomadic—but independent—existence. He moved several times—from the meatless table of Monsignor Pandolfo Pucci, who was the first to house him, to the Consolazione hospital when he fell ill with malaria, and then to the studio of Giuseppe d'Arpino, a fashionable artist of the time. But at last he was to enjoy the generous hospitality of his chief protector, Cardinal del Monte.

The first small canvases which Caravaggio executed in Rome were of an aggressive and controversial nature, and his models were depicted either as Bacchus or St John the Baptist, posed as if intent on keeping balance or as if they were about to taste the fruit before them. These characteristics are first apparent in the angry and crude renderings of well-known themes of sixteenth-century court classicism, and in the radical nature of his composition, which rejected every established convention. He did not think it necessary to take into account anything that was not immediately apparent to him, and only included that which he actually saw. Thus he expressed himself in terms of "inexorable naturalness" in his late works.

It is easy to understand how extremely threatening such new freedom in pictorial vision seemed to the followers of Humanism, which by now had lost its moral content and was relegated to the position of a clumsy academic *mise en scène*. At that very time the classical world was making a last attempt to save its dignity and to preserve its civilization in the collective undertaking of the frescos in the Salon of the Borghese Palace, but it was strongly opposed by the *fronde* of young artists who were drawn to the bold naturalism of Caravaggio, who explicitly affirmed that "he took as much trouble to paint a canvas of flowers as he did a human figure."

In the beginning only a few noticed the revolutionary principle on which Caravaggio's art was based. The hour of official recognition awaited the completion, in about 1598, of the three canvases comprising episodes from the Story of St Matthew (plates 24, 25 and 32) which had been commissioned for San Luigi dei Francesi. Then the battle began! However, during his first years in Rome, when he was forced to live on the little received from uncertain profits of small pictures which he had painted specifically "to sell," he still wavered irresolutely between his "first soft and pure manner of painting," and the second one which was severe and plastically robust. Caravaggio's fame could not have traveled far outside the circle of private patrons and the collectors with keener taste, who were always searching for "delightful" and extravagant "pieces," although they were too often inclined to appreciate the literary subject of the painting rather than the work itself. In fact at this time even Caravaggio practised genre painting, in the manner of

Giorgione, as is apparent in the *Fortune Teller*, the *Cardsharps*, the *Narcissus*, and the *Concert* (plates 9, 10, 11 and 19). This latter work was executed for Cardinal del Monte and then lost; Caravaggio himself considered it "the finest thing he ever did." However, this genre work, which met with easy success, did not interrupt his "direct painting," which expressed ideas beyond those he had merely learned. Of this type of work we find examples in the same period, such as the *Bacchus* (plate 5) in the Uffizi, the *Boy with a Basket of Fruit* (plate 1) in the Borghese Gallery, *The Sick Bacchus*—certainly a self-portrait—also in the Borghese Gallery. All these works can be described in modern terms as more or less "from a sitting model."

In effect, another work painted "from a sitting" model was the *Mary Magdalen* (plate 17) in the Doria Gallery. Bellori's *Life* tells us: "he painted a girl seated on a chair, with her hands on her breast, in the act of drying her hair. Then he put a room in as background, added a vase of ointment on the ground, some necklaces and gems, and pretended that it was Mary Magdalen." In this work, which is clearly based on his own theoretical ideas and which brings to mind Lotto and Salvoldo, Caravaggio shows that he had passed from the festive chromatic clarity of the group of works executed around 1590-2, among which the idyllic *Rest during the Flight into Egypt* (plate 15), the gem of the Doria Gallery, is outstanding—to a new and more dramatic synthesis of form and light, which we find in his paintings of interiors where the model stands out powerfully against the bare background of a room in deep shadow.

Light now grows in importance in Caravaggio's painting and no more obstacles prevent its development. Light falls on the objects, takes them by surprise, and fixes their solid consistency. Life is created from the charm of the solidity, color and fire of the light; where it grows thin and dies away, thick patches of shadow spread out. These stylistic concepts are culminated in the masterpiece of this period: the grand paintings of the Contarelli Chapel at San Luigi dei Francesi, executed between 1590 and 1598. The first version of that altarpiece, with St Matthew and the Angel, was refused by the clergy due to their falsely moralistic scruples. It was preserved in Berlin until 1945 when, along with some of his other works, it was lost in a fire which destroyed a shelter for works of art. Despite scandal, this meant official recognition for the Lombard master. With this cycle of San Luigi dei Francesi, a new order of painting was truly inaugurated, destined to grow in strength. It exerted influence on those who directly followed Caravaggio, but even more so on Velazquez, Rembrandt and Vermeer; moreover, it foreshadowed nineteenth-century French Impressionism. It is important to bear in mind that Caravaggio achieved this not through the use of spirited "stage scenery" painted against the light in the style of the great "producer," Tintoretto, but by means of his own intransigent and original naturalism.

Caravaggio took approximately eight years to finish the paintings in the Contarelli Chapel. We can date also other works of great importance as being executed in this same period: the powerful *Supper at Emmaus* in London (plate 41) which depicts definite and grave gestures vividly cleaving space; *The Incredulity of St Thomas* (plate 53) with its closed, circular composition, and the *Holy Family*, the *Crowning with Thorns*, and the *Seizure of Christ by Night*, all three of which are unfortunately only known to us through copies. More and more critics began to praise his work and to emphasize the integrity, the coherence, and the fullness of moral feeling which he showed. He was now rich in experience; he now felt the urge to look harsh reality in the face and to throw himself into life with the fierce and impassioned force of an apostle.

The first years of the seventeenth century, therefore, saw the creation of the bitter and apparently revolutionary canvases of Santa Maria del Popolo (Cerasi Chapel): the *Crucifixion of St Peter* (plate 48), in which the choking, groveling bodies seem to lack breathing space; the bold *Conversion of St Paul* (plate 49), in which the great horse seems to play the part of protagonist in a destiny beyond human control. Caravaggio's plastic luminosity here attains its greatest vigor and warmth.

In contrast, the severe *Burial of Christ* (plate 59) in the Vatican, which was long considered the artist's masterpiece, seems to retire into a statuesque gravity and an atmosphere similar to Michelangelo's—even the play of light is less dramatic and seems to be slower. On the other hand, the living stele that is the Virgin in the *Madonna of the Pilgrims* (or *of Loreto*) in the Church of Sant' Agostino in Rome (plate 56) deserves praise precisely because its very existence seems to be in light; its visionary reality is accentuated by the two naturalistic figures of the devout at the base, who form a markedly engaging contrast.

Caravaggio's classic phase soon comes to an end (after the fascinating *Love Victorious* at Berlin) in the strongly drawn *Madonna of the Palafrenieri* (or *of the Serpent*), executed for the altar of the Confraternity of the Grooms (*Palafrenieri*) in St Peter's at Rome (plate 64). However, it was not placed there because the rounded, naked body of the Child was thought to resemble a Hellenistic cupid, and was consequently judged immodest. This is but one of many such episodes in the irregular and turbulent existence which Caravaggio's fierce and biting nature caused him to lead. He was associated with the ringleaders of scandal in the restless bohemian life of Rome, one of whom was his friend, the architect Onorio Longhi. Caravaggio's was an adventurous nature. He had the tongue of a viper, and was always ready to engage in brawls or rows and nightly skirmishes. These almost inevitably ended up before a magistrate, to whom the artist was brought by the police—who frequently first acquainted him with the harshness of the *Tor di Nona* prison. From 1601 to 1605, the archives of various courts of justice in Rome often reveal the name of Caravaggio. Sometimes it was because of a quarrel between rival artists, as in the suit for slander brought against him in 1603 by Baglione, his future biographer; other times it was because of a woman; yet other times it was because of a tavern brawl or for the use of weapons in street-corner quarrels, or on the playing field. Someone always intervened in his favor and furnished bail or guarantees: work companions, fellow artists, illustrious prelates, or diplomats who were accredited at the court of Rome. This anything but agreeable prodigal son had many friends: persons such as Cardinal del Monte, the Doria, and the Giustiniani families hastened to prove their loyalty to him by buying the canvases which were refused in horror by the clergy, who did not and could not understand the artist's invincible freedom of mind.

Caravaggio was anxious to be considered a man of honor: one whose fundamental honesty could not be doubted. So he faced these misadventures with *bravura*. However, they became too frequent and matters came to a climax in 1605: the artist wounded a lawyer, Mariano Pasqualone, who had unsuccessfully courted the peasant girl used as a model for the *Madonna of the Pilgrims*. Caravaggio was pardoned, but shortly thereafter, during a ball game, he had a fight with Rannuccio Tommasoni and killed him. To avoid the police, he was obliged to flee Rome and, as if this was not enough, the serious scandal of the *Death of the Virgin* (plate 65) broke at this time. The picture had been painted for the Church of Santa Maria della Scala. When it was exhibited a rumor was circulated to the effect that Caravaggio had acted in a sacrilegious manner, for in the figure of the Madonna herself the public recognized a prostitute whose body had been fished out of the Tiber only a few days before. Artists bowed in wonder before this work, which is one—if not the greatest—of Caravaggio's works: it is a spectacular representation of restraint in intense grief, portrayed in tragic and solitary light. Once more, a work had to be removed from the altar: it was secretly sold to the Duke of Mantua and is now in the Louvre.

Difficult and depressing years in exile, wandering from place to place, now followed. We hear of the artist next in Genoa, in 1605. The following year, after a brief return to Rome where he was temporarily readmitted due to the leniency of Pope Paul V, he took lodgings at near-by Pagliano, under the illusion that he might be able to obtain another pardon. He continued painting, since his influential Roman protectors supported him with commissions for new works, among which was the second *Supper at Emmaus* (plate 69) which is now at the Brera. But these works reveal Caravaggio's despairing pessimism and mental distress. In the *David and Goliath* and the *St Jerome* (plates 77 and 73) in the Borghese Gallery, the theme of death recurs with tragic insistence. The execution is more summary; it now depends completely on an implacably shining, violent, almost savage light.

By the end of 1606, Caravaggio had concluded that the permission to return to Rome for which he had so long hoped, would never arrive. He went to Naples, where he executed the angry and rather turbid *Scourging of Christ* (plate 78) in San Domenico Maggiore, and the careless but inspired canvas of the *Seven Works of Mercy* (plate 84). In Naples, too, he left a notable statement of religious feeling, executed in a mature and monumental style: this was the *Madonna of the Rosary* (plate 80). In this work, the idea expressed in the *Madonna of the Pilgrims* in Rome is repeated and expanded in a grand manner: the softened light creates the best possible effect in the flesh of the strongly archi-tectonic figures. But this stay in Naples—where his work had deep influence—was only one episode in the wandering existence that constituted Caravaggio's last years. In 1608 he was welcomed in Malta with honor by the Grand Master of the Order of Malta, Alof de Wignacourt, of whom the artist did two portraits (the one in which De Wignacourt is standing with a servant who bears a plumed helmet, is usually identified with the painting now in the Louvre). It is probably to De Wignacourt that Caravaggio owed the com-mission for religious works for the cathedral of Valletta: the *Beheading of John the Baptist* and a *St Jerome* (plates 88 and 89).

Again, this was only a brief interval of well-being. Soon he quarreled with another knight over the administration of justice (Caravaggio had been knighted in 1608), was thrown into prison and lost the Grand Master's favor forever. He escaped but was pursued by cut-throats who were under orders to kill him. Thereafter, he was continually fleeing from them. We know he stopped at Syracuse, Messina, and Palermo; in all three cities he left behind works of great importance. Except, however, in the *Adoration of the Shep-herds* at Messina (plate 94), signs of weariness are evident in all of them, and the execution is hasty and careless. These last works show that the Lombard genius, who now bore the reputation of a criminal, rarely found peace again.

Although he had escaped with his life from attack by the assassins in Naples, they had left him badly cut about the face; therefore he took a ship for Rome. When he landed north of Rome, he was mistakenly arrested, then released. Stricken with malarial fever, he dragged himself, in desperation, on to the beach at Porto Ercole near Grosseto. Deprived of all aid, he died there on July 18, 1610. Ten days later the news was announced at the Papal court: "Word has been received of the death of Michel Angelo Caravaggio, the famous painter, who was so outstanding in painting and drawing from nature. . . ."

# BIOGRAPHICAL NOTES

1573, SEPTEMBER 28. Michelangelo Merisi, son of Fermo, is born at Caravaggio in the region of Bergamo.

1584–8. Caravaggio spends four years in Milan in the school of the painter Simone Peterzano.

1589 (circa). He goes to Rome (Mancini, his biographer, speaks of "the twenty-year-old Caravaggio"), where he stays with Monsignor Pandolfo Pucci. He becomes ill and is taken to the Consolazione Hospital. Later he collaborates with Giuseppe d'Arpino.

1598. Consecration of the Contarelli Chapel in the Church of San Luigi dei Francesi at Rome, in which are the paintings of the life of St Matthew, that Caravaggio had begun about eight years before.

1600 (circa). Execution of two canvases, Crucifixion of St Peter and The Conversion of St Paul, for the Cerasi Chapel in the Church of Santa Maria del Popolo at Rome.

1603. The artist Giovanni Baglione brings an action for slander against the artists Michelangelo da Caravaggio, Orazio Gentileschi, Filippo Trisegni, and the architect Onorio Longhi, a close friend of Caravaggio.

1604. Caravaggio is commissioned at Tolentino to execute an altar-piece for the high altar of the Capuchin church.

1604. Caravaggio's Burial of Christ is placed above the altar of the Church of Santa Maria della Vallicella at Rome. About the same time, he paints the Madonna of the Pilgrims for the Church of Sant'Agostino.

1605. Caravaggio seriously wounds a notary, Mariano Pasqualone, and is forced to flee from Rome. He is in Genoa in August but, at the end of the month, he is permitted to return to Rome.

1606, MAY 31. Caravaggio kills Rannuccio Tommasoni from Teramo in a quarrel on the Campo Marzio. Once again, he is obliged to flee the city to escape arrest. In September he is at work on various commissions in Pagliano, near Rome. He goes to Naples, probably toward the end of the year.

1607. The painter, Pourbus, in a letter to the Duke of Mantua, mentions seeing the Madonna of the Rosary and a Judith and Holofernes in the collection of the Prince of Conca at Naples, both executed by Caravaggio.

1608. Caravaggio is in Malta at the invitation of the Grand Master of the Order, Alof de Wignacourt, and is knighted there. However, at the end of the year he quarrels with another Knight of the Order and is imprisoned. He escapes and goes to Syracuse, where he paints the *Burial of St Lucy*.

1609. Caravaggio paints the *Raising of Lazarus* and the *Adoration of the Shepherds* at Messina. A little later, in Palermo, he paints the *Nativity with SS Laurence and Francis*. He returns to Naples, where he is gravely wounded by de Wignacourt's assassins.

1610, JULY 18. He dies of malaria, abandoned by all, on the beach of Porto Ercole near Grosseto, while on his way to Rome.

# CARAVAGGIO'S PAINTINGS

### Color Plate I
THE SICK BACCHUS.

### Plate 1
BOY WITH A BASKET OF FRUIT.
*Oil on canvas, 70 × 67.\* Rome,
Borghese Gallery.* This, and the works
reproduced in plates 2 and 5, belong
to the group of little canvases which
Mancini says Caravaggio executed
"to sell" at the beginning of his stay
in Rome. Dated *circa* 1589.

### Plate 2
THE SICK BACCHUS or SELF-
PORTRAIT AS BACCHUS. *Oil on
canvas, 66 × 52. Rome, Borghese
Gallery.* According to Longhi, this
can be related to the time when
Caravaggio was in hospital with
malaria; that is, around 1590.

### Plate 3
BOY BITTEN BY A LIZARD. *Oil on
canvas, 66 × 34. Florence, Roberto
Longhi Collection.* Mentioned by
Baglione and Mancini. Of particular
interest because of the boy's expres-
sion of mimicry. (See also plate 4.)

### Plate 4
BOY BITTEN BY A LIZARD, detail.
Still life.

### Plate 5
BACCHUS. *Oil on canvas, 95 × 85.
Florence, Uffizi Gallery.* Presumably,
this work may be identified as the
artist's early Roman work, after his
stay with D'Arpino, which Baglione
records. About 1589. (See also
plates 6–7.)

### Plate 6
BACCHUS, detail. Hand with goblet.

### Plate 7
BACCHUS, detail. Face of Bacchus.

### Plate 8
THE LUTE PLAYER. *Oil on canvas,
94 × 114. Leningrad, Hermitage.*
Executed about 1590, for Cardinal
del Monte, and passed by him to
the Marchese Vincenzo Giustiniani.
Mentioned by Baglione and Bellori.
Dated *circa* 1590.

### Plate 9
THE CONCERT. *Oil on canvas, 92 ×
118.5. New York, Metropolitan Museum
of Art.* Recently discovered by Denis
Mahon in a private English collection. After an effort was made to
clean it, he compared it with other
similar paintings from Caravaggio's
first period in Rome, and identified it
with *"Several boys making music,
painted from nature and very well
done"*, which Bellori noted in the
collection of Cardinal del Monte.
(See Lost Paintings, under the same
title.) Longhi confirmed the attribution to Caravaggio, but excludes
the above-mentioned identification,
because of the "unrealistic tone of
the painting" and "its insolent
pagan allegorism". The work can be
dated around 1590.

* All dimensions are given in centimeters.

## Plate 10

THE FORTUNE TELLER (*Buona Ventura*). *Oil on canvas, 99 × 131. Paris, Louvre.* With the *Lute Player* (plate 8) and the *Cardsharps* (*I Bari*) (plate 11), this work belongs to the number of genre subjects executed in the manner of Giorgione, at half-length, mentioned by Caravaggio's first biographers (Baglione, Mancini, Bellori) as being among his earliest Roman works. (See also plate 12.)

## Plate 11

THE CARDSHARPS (*I Bari*). *Oil on canvas, 99 × 137.* This work was described by Bellori and was formerly in the Barberini Gallery in Rome, whence it passed to the Sciarra Collection. It later became part of the Rothschild Collection in Paris. Today its whereabouts are unknown. (See also plate 13.)

## Plate 12

THE FORTUNE TELLER, detail. The gipsy woman.

## Plate 13

THE CARDSHARPS, detail. Bust of a player.

## Plate 14

ECSTASY OF ST FRANCIS. *Oil on canvas, 91 × 128. Hartford, Massachusetts, Wadsworth Atheneum.* Perhaps to be identified with the painting mentioned in the will of Ruggero Tritonio, Abbot of Pinerolo, in 1597. *Circa* 1594.

## Plate 15

REST DURING THE FLIGHT INTO EGYPT. *Oil on canvas, 130 × 160. Rome, Doria Gallery.* Mentioned by Mancini and Bellori. This work is all-important for an understanding of the Brescian-Bergamescan influences on the young Caravaggio. *Circa* 1590. (See also plate 16.)

## Plate 16

REST DURING THE FLIGHT INTO EGYPT, detail. Background landscape.

## Color Plate II

MEDUSA.

## Plate 17

MARY MAGDALEN. *Oil on canvas, 106 × 97. Rome, Doria Gallery.* Mentioned by Mancini and Bellori. This work is particularly significant for the new synthesis of plastic and light elements, toward which Caravaggio began to move after his earliest Roman period.

## Plate 18

ST JOHN THE BAPTIST. *Oil on canvas, 132 × 95. Rome, Doria Gallery.* Mentioned by Bellori. There are clear reminders of the nudes by Michelangelo in the Sistine Chapel. This is a youthful work.

## Plate 19

NARCISSUS. *Oil on canvas, 110 × 92. Rome, Galleria Nazionale d'Arte Antica.* This work is the one that most reflects the influence of the painter Savoldo on Caravaggio. Some scholars cast doubt on its authenticity.

## Plate 20

PORTRAIT OF A WOMAN. *Oil on canvas, 66 × 53.* Formerly in Berlin, Kaiser Friedrich Museum, this work was destroyed in 1945. Some have wished to identify the subject of the portrait with Margherita Campani, who is mentioned by early writers.

### Plate 21

ST CATHERINE. *Oil on canvas, 173 × 133. Lugano, Schloss Rohoncz Foundation.* Formerly in the Barberini Gallery. Bellori says that it was executed for Cardinal del Monte. *Circa* 1592.

### Plate 22

ST MATTHEW AND THE ANGEL. *Oil on canvas, 223 × 183.* Formerly in Berlin, Kaiser Friedrich Museum, this work was destroyed in 1945. This is the painting originally intended for the altar of the Contarelli Chapel in the Church of San Luigi dei Francesi at Rome, which was refused by the clergy. It then passed into the collection of Marchese Vicenzo Giustiniani. *Circa* 1590. (See also plate 23.)

### Plate 23

ST MATTHEW AND THE ANGEL, detail. Busts of the Saint and angel.

### Plate 24

THE CALLING OF ST MATTHEW. *Oil on canvas, 315 × 315. Rome, Church of San Luigi dei Francesi.* Commissioned by Cardinal Cointrel for his family chapel in the church, at the recommendation of Cardinal del Monte. The execution of the three canvases of the life of St Matthew can reasonably be placed between 1590 and 1598. Noteworthy in the group of players is the close correlation with genre subjects in the manner of the *Cardsharps* (plate 13). The malevolent comment of Federico Zuccari reported by Baglione, to the effect that there was nothing to be seen in the whole of the series but "the ideas of Giorgione," seems to refer particularly to this canvas. The work may be dated 1592–5. (See also plates 26–8.)

### Plate 25

THE MARTYRDOM OF ST MATTHEW. *Oil on canvas, 315 × 315. Rome, Church of San Luigi dei Francesi.* The composition is based on the effect of accentuated dramatic movement. *Circa* 1592–5. (See also plates 29–31.)

### Plate 26

THE CALLING OF ST MATTHEW, detail of left side. Matthew answers the call of the Redeemer.

### Plate 27

THE CALLING OF ST MATTHEW, detail of the right side. The Redeemer signals Matthew to follow Him.

### Plate 28

THE CALLING OF ST MATTHEW, detail from the center. A group of young men.

### Plate 29

THE MARTYRDOM OF ST MATTHEW, detail from the center. The Saint and his executioners.

### Plate 30

THE MARTYRDOM OF ST MATTHEW, detail from the right. Frightened boy.

### Plate 31

THE MARTYRDOM OF ST MATTHEW, detail of the background. Self-portrait of Caravaggio.

### Plate 32

ST MATTHEW AND THE ANGEL. *Oil on canvas, 295 × 195. Rome, Church of San Luigi dei Francesi.* It is probable that this was the last to be delivered of the three canvases forming this important group.

## Plate 33

THE CONVERSION OF ST PAUL. *Oil on canvas, 237 × 189. Rome, Odescalchi Balbi Collection.* Like the *Ecstasy of St Francis* (plate 14), it reflects the lively Lombard naturalism in which Caravaggio was first trained.

## Plate 34

THE CONVERSION OF ST PAUL, detail. Christ and an angel.

## Plate 35

THE SACRIFICE OF ISAAC. *Oil on canvas, 104 × 135. Florence, Uffizi.* According to Bellori it was painted for Maffeo Barberini. A youthful work, the authenticity of which is questioned by some. (See also plates 36–7.)

## Plate 36

THE SACRIFICE OF ISAAC, detail. Background landscape.

## Plate 37

THE SACRIFICE OF ISAAC, detail. Hand with knife.

## Plate 38

LOVE VICTORIOUS. *Oil on canvas, 154 × 110. Berlin, Staatliche Museen.* Painted for Marchese Vincenzo Giustiniani. It is mentioned in the records of the lawsuit brought against Caravaggio by Baglione in 1603. (See also plate 39.)

## Plate 39

LOVE VICTORIOUS, detail. Still life.

## Plate 40

MEDUSA. *Oil on canvas, attached to a round convex board with a diameter of 55. Florence, Uffizi.* According to Baglione it was painted as a shield for a tournament, commissioned by Cardinal del Monte, who in 1608 sent it as a gift to Cosimo II, Grand Duke of Tuscany.

## Plate 41

THE SUPPER AT EMMAUS. *Oil on canvas, 139 × 195. London, National Gallery.* Mentioned by Baglione and Bellori. *Circa* 1594–5. (See also plates 42–6.)

## Plate 42

THE SUPPER AT EMMAUS, detail. A disciple.

## Plate 43

THE SUPPER AT EMMAUS, detail. The other disciple.

## Plate 44

THE SUPPER AT EMMAUS, detail. The breaking of the bread.

## Plate 45

THE SUPPER AT EMMAUS, detail. Head of Christ.

## Plate 46

THE SUPPER AT EMMAUS, detail. Still life.

## Plate 47

BASKET OF FRUIT. *Oil on canvas, 45 × 59. Milan, Pinacoteca Ambrosiana.* Sent as a gift in 1596 by Cardinal del Monte to Federico Borromeo for his gallery at Milan.

## Plate 48

THE CRUCIFIXION OF ST PETER. *Oil on canvas, 230 × 175. Rome, Cerasi Chapel in the Church of Santa Maria del Popolo.* Executed at the same time as the *Conversion of St Paul* (plate 49), *circa* 1601–2. Both works are fundamental to the artist's full maturity.

## Plate 49

THE CONVERSION OF ST PAUL. *Oil on canvas, 230 × 175. Rome, Cerasi Chapel in the Church of Santa Maria del Popolo. Circa* 1601–2. (See also plates 50–1.)

## Plate 50

THE CONVERSION OF ST PAUL, detail. St Paul lying on the ground.

## Plate 51

THE CONVERSION OF ST PAUL, detail. Heads of the groom and horse.

## Plate 52

ST JOHN THE BAPTIST. *Oil on canvas, 99 × 145. Rome, Galleria Nazionale d'Arte Antica.* Datable about the turn of the sixteenth century.

## Plate 53

THE INCREDULITY OF ST THOMAS. *Oil on canvas, 107 × 146.* Formerly at Potsdam, in the Neues Palais; now probably lost. Originally it was in the collection of Marchese Giustiniani, and was mentioned by Baglione and Bellori. *Circa* 1595. Its authenticity is disputed.

## Plate 54

ST FRANCIS. *Oil on canvas, 128 × 94. Rome, Convent of the Capuchins. Circa* 1598.

## Plate 55

ST JOHN THE BAPTIST. *Oil on canvas, 172 × 134. English private collection.* Datable about the beginning of the seventeenth century.

## Plate 56

MADONNA OF THE PILGRIMS (or OF LORETO). *Oil on canvas, 260 × 150. Rome, Church of Sant'Agostino. Circa* 1603–4. (See also plates 57–8.)

## Plate 57

MADONNA OF THE PILGRIMS, detail: the two pilgrims.

## Plate 58

MADONNA OF THE PILGRIMS, detail. Madonna and Child.

## Plate 59

BURIAL OF CHRIST. *Oil on canvas, 300 × 203. Rome, Pinacoteca Vaticana.* Originally executed for the Church of Santa Maria in Vallicella. The work may be dated between 1602 and 1604. It is traditionally regarded as Caravaggio's masterpiece. (See also plates 60–1.)

## Plate 60

BURIAL OF CHRIST, detail. Christ's body.

## Color Plate III

ST JEROME.

## Plate 61

BURIAL OF CHRIST, detail. Group of mourners.

## Plate 62

CHRIST ON THE MOUNT OF OLIVES. *Oil on canvas, 154 × 222.* Formerly in Berlin, Kaiser Friedrich Museum, but destroyed in 1945. Of the same period as the *Incredulity of*

*St Thomas* (plate 53). By some critics, this work is not regarded as authentic. (See also plate 63.)

## Plate 63

CHRIST ON THE MOUNT OF OLIVES, detail. Sleeping Apostle.

## Plate 64

MADONNA OF THE PALAFRENIERI (or OF THE SERPENT). *Oil on canvas, 292 × 211. Rome, Borghese Gallery.* Commissioned by the Confraternity of the Grooms (*Palafrenieri*) for its altar in St Peter's, but rejected by the clergy on moralistic grounds. The work was then given to Cardinal Borghese. *Circa* 1605–6.

## Plate 65

DEATH OF THE VIRGIN. *Oil on canvas, 369 × 245. Paris, Louvre.* Painted for the Church of Santa Maria della Scala, but rejected for mistaken reasons of decorum. The work was then acquired for the gallery of the Duke of Mantua, whence it passed in 1627 to the collection of Charles I of England. *Circa* 1605. (See also plates 66–8.)

## Plate 66

DEATH OF THE VIRGIN, detail. Weeping child.

## Plate 67

DEATH OF THE VIRGIN, detail. Head of the Virgin.

## Plate 68

DEATH OF THE VIRGIN, detail. Group of Apostles.

## Plate 69

THE SUPPER AT EMMAUS. Oil on canvas, 145 × 195. Milan, Brera Gallery (collection of the Marchese Patrizi of Rome). This is a repetition, with noteworthy variations, of the *Supper at Emmaus* in London (plate 41). This work was painted *circa* 1605. (See also plates 70–1.)

## Plate 70

THE SUPPER AT EMMAUS, detail. Christ.

## Plate 71

THE SUPPER AT EMMAUS, detail. The host and maid-servant.

## Plate 72

DAVID AND GOLIATH. *Oil on board, 95 × 165. Vienna, Kunsthistorisches Museum.* The work was painted during the last years of the artist's stay in Rome.

## Plate 73

ST JEROME. *Oil on canvas, 112 × 157. Rome, Borghese Gallery.* According to Bellori, painted for Cardinal Scipione Borghese. Together with the *David and Goliath* (plate 77), it belongs to the years 1604–6, the times of Caravaggio's flight from Rome and subsequent exile at Pagliano. (See also plate 74 and color plate III.)

## Plate 74

ST JEROME, detail.

## Plate 75

ST JEROME. *Oil on canvas, 100 × 81. Barcelona, Monastery of Montserrat.* Painted in the late Roman period, about 1603.

## Plate 76

ST JOHN THE BAPTIST. *Oil on canvas, 150 × 122. Rome, Borghese*

*Gallery*. A late repetition of a theme already treated several times by Caravaggio.

## Color Plate IV
ST JOHN THE BAPTIST.

## Plate 77
DAVID AND GOLIATH. *Oil on canvas, 125 × 91. Rome, Borghese Gallery.* In agreement with the early biographers, the head of Goliath is regarded as a self-portrait of the artist. The work should be dated 1605-6.

## Plate 78
THE SCOURGING OF CHRIST. *Oil on canvas, 300 × 230. Naples, Church of San Domenico Maggiore.* Mentioned by Bellori. Executed at Naples in 1607. (See also plate 79.)

## Plate 79
THE SCOURGING OF CHRIST, detail. Christ.

## Plate 80
MADONNA OF THE ROSARY. *Oil on canvas, 346 × 249. Vienna, Kunsthistorisches Museum.* Pourbus describes it in a letter to the Duke of Mantua in 1607. Mentioned in the will of the artist Finsonius in 1607. It was later in the Church of the Dominicans at Antwerp, whence in 1781, it was acquired by Joseph II of Austria. This is the masterpiece of the artist's Neapolitan period. (See also plates 81-2.)

## Plate 81
MADONNA OF THE ROSARY, detail. Madonna and Child.

## Plate 82
MADONNA OF THE ROSARY, detail. The faithful paying homage, and a portrait of the donor of the picture to the church.

## Plate 83
SALOME WITH THE HEAD OF JOHN THE BAPTIST. *Oil on canvas, 116 × 140. Madrid, The Escorial, Casita del Principe.* To be assigned to the artist's Neapolitan period (1607). The attribution to Caravaggio was recently confirmed by Longhi.

## Plate 84
THE SEVEN WORKS OF MERCY. *Oil on canvas, 390 × 260. Naples, Pio Monte della Misericordia.* Mentioned by Bellori. Like Caravaggio's other Neapolitan works, this was executed in 1607. (See also plates 85-6.)

## Plate 85
THE SEVEN WORKS OF MERCY, detail. Left side.

## Plate 86
THE SEVEN WORKS OF MERCY, detail. Madonna and angels.

## Plate 87
SLEEPING CUPID. *Oil on canvas, 71 × 105. Florence, Pitti Palace.* According to an old inscription on the back, the painting was executed when the artist was in Malta (1608).

## Plate 88
BEHEADING OF JOHN THE BAPTIST. *Oil on canvas, 361 × 520. Malta, Valletta, Cathedral of St John the Baptist.* Mentioned by Bellori.

## Plate 89
ST JEROME. *Oil on canvas, 117 × 157. Malta, Valletta, Cathedral of St John the Baptist.* Mentioned by Bellori.

## Plate 90
ALOF DE WIGNACOURT, GRAND MASTER OF THE ORDER OF MALTA. *Oil on canvas, 195 × 134. Paris, Louvre.* Traditionally regarded as

one of the two portraits of de Wignacourt that Bellori records among the artist's Maltese works (1608). Recently, there have been doubts about the attribution of the work.

### Plate 91

BURIAL OF ST LUCY. *Oil on canvas, 408 × 300. Syracuse, Church of Santa Lucia.* Mentioned by Bellori. *Circa* 1608. Damaged by early restoration. (See also plate 92.)

### Plate 92

BURIAL OF ST LUCY, detail. The mourners.

### Plate 93

THE RAISING OF LAZARUS. *Oil on canvas, 380 × 275. Messina, Museo Nazionale.* Painted for the Church of the Crociferi, and commissioned by Giovanni Battista de Lazzari. Dated 1608–9.

### Plate 94

ADORATION OF THE SHEPHERDS. *Oil on canvas, 304 × 217. Messina, Museo Nazionale.* Painted in 1609 for the Capuchin church at Messina. Mentioned by Bellori. (See also plate 95.)

### Plate 95

ADORATION OF THE SHEPHERDS, detail. The shepherds.

### Plate 96

NATIVITY WITH SS LAURENCE AND FRANCIS. *Oil on canvas, 268 × 197. Palermo, Oratory of San Lorenzo.* Mentioned by Bellori. This is Caravaggio's last known work.

# LOST PAINTINGS

BOY PEELING A PEAR WITH A KNIFE. Mentioned by Mancini. There are copies at Hampton Court and in the Longhi Collection at Florence.

CONCERT. Mentioned by Baglione as in the possession of Cardinal del Monte. (See also plate 9.)

CAPTURE OF CHRIST IN THE GARDEN. Mentioned by Baglione, and on several occasions by Bellori.

ECCE HOMO. Painted, according to Bellori, at Rome, and commissioned by the Massimo family.

JUDITH AND HOLOFERNES. Baglione says this work was executed for the Costa family at Rome. It later passed into the Conca Collection at Naples, where Pourbus noted it.

THE WALK TO EMMAUS. According to Bellori, executed for Ciriaco Mattei. Various copies are known. An engraved reproduction was made by Murphy.

THE CROWNING WITH THORNS. Executed for Marchese Giustiniani (Bellori).

PORTRAIT OF ONORIO LONGHI. Mentioned in the will of the architect Martino Longhi.

MARY MAGDALEN. According to Bellori, this work was commissioned by Marzio Colonna.

THE CRUCIFIXION OF ST ANDREW. In Bellori's time this work was in Spain and there is a copy in the Museum of Toledo. Another copy is in the Bach Vega Collection in Vienna. (See Attributed Paintings.)

THE RESURRECTION. Formerly in the Church of Sant'Anna dei Lombardi at Naples. Mentioned by Mancini.

# PAINTINGS ATTRIBUTED TO CARAVAGGIO

STILL LIFE. *Washington, D.C., National Gallery (Samuel H. Kress Foundation).* Attribution by R. Longhi.

THE FORTUNE TELLER. *Rome, Capitol Gallery.* Traditionally held to be a reproduction with variations of *The Fortune Teller* now in the Louvre. (See plate 10.)

PORTRAIT OF MAFFEO BARBERINI. *Florence, Corsini Gallery.* Attribution by L. Venturi.

LUTE PLAYER. *Munich, Kunstsammlung des Bayerischen Staätes.* Attribution by R. Longhi. When it was in the museum at Augsburg it was designated "German School."

PORTRAIT OF POPE PAUL V. *Rome, Borghese Collection.* Attribution by L. Venturi.

DAVID AND GOLIATH. *Madrid, Prado.* Attribution by A. Venturi.

JUDITH AND HOLOFERNES. *Rome, Private Collection.* Attribution by R. Longhi.

CHRIST ON THE WAY TO CALVARY. *Vienna, Kunsthistorisches Museum.* Attribution by R. Longhi. (In the museum it was designated "Battistello Caracciolo.")

ECCE HOMO. *Genoa, Museum of Palazzo Bianco.* Attribution by R. Longhi.

ST JOHN THE BAPTIST. *Basel, Oeffentliche Kunstsammlung.* Attribution by A. Venturi.

THE HOLY FAMILY WITH THE YOUNG ST JOHN THE BAPTIST. *Berlin, Staatliche Museen.* Attribution by H. Voss.

CRUCIFIXION OF ST ANDREW. *Vienna, Bach Vega Collection.* Attribution by G. Fiocco.

THE SUPPER AT EMMAUS. *Messina, Museo Nazionale.* Attribution by R. Longhi. (In the museum it is attributed to "A. Rodriguez.")

THE INCREDULITY OF ST THOMAS. *Messina, Museo Nazionale.* Attribution by R. Longhi. (In the museum it is attributed to "A. Rodriguez.")

# LOCATION OF PAINTINGS

**BERLIN**

STAATLICHE MUSEEN
*Love Victorious* (plates 38, 39).

**FLORENCE**

PITTI PALACE
*Sleeping Cupid* (plate 87).

UFFIZI GALLERY
*Bacchus* (plates 5, 6, 7).
*Medusa* (plate 40 and color plate II).
*The Sacrifice of Isaac* (plates 35, 36, 37).

LONGHI COLLECTION
*Boy Bitten by a Lizard* (plates 3, 4).

**HARTFORD (MASSACHUSETTS)**

WADSWORTH ATHENEUM
*Ecstasy of St Francis* (plate 14).

**LENINGRAD**

HERMITAGE
*The Lute Player* (plate 8).

**LONDON**

NATIONAL GALLERY
*The Supper at Emmaus* (plates 41, 42, 43, 44, 45, 46).

**LUGANO**

SCHLOSS ROHONCZ FOUNDATION
*St Catherine* (plate 21).

**MADRID**

THE ESCORIAL (CASITA DEL PRINCIPE)
*Salome with the Head of John the Baptist* (plate 83).

**MESSINA**

MUSEO NAZIONALE
*The Raising of Lazarus* (plate 93).
*Adoration of the Shepherds* (plates 94, 95).

**MILAN**

PINACOTECA AMBROSIANA
*Basket of Fruit* (plate 47).

BRERA GALLERY
*The Supper at Emmaus* (plates 69, 70, 71).

**MONTSERRAT (BARCELONA)**

THE MONASTERY
*St Jerome* (plate 75).

**NAPLES**

CHURCH OF SAN DOMENICO MAGGIORE
*The Scourging of Christ* (plates 78, 79).

PIO MONTE DELLA MISERICORDIA
*The Seven Works of Mercy* (plates 84, 85, 86).

## NEW YORK

METROPOLITAN MUSEUM OF
ART
*The Concert* (plate 9).

## PALERMO

THE ORATORY OF SAN
LORENZO
*Nativity with SS Laurence and
Francis* (plate 96).

## PARIS

LOUVRE
*The Fortune Teller* (plates 10, 12).
*Death of the Virgin* (plates 65, 66,
67, 68).
*Alof de Wignacourt* (plate 90).

## ROME

BORGHESE GALLERY
*Boy with a Basket of Fruit* (plate 1).
*The Sick Bacchus* (plate 2 and color
plate I).
*Madonna of the Palafrenieri* (or
*of the Serpent*) (plate 64).
*St Jerome* (plates 73, 74 and color
plate III).
*St John the Baptist* (plate 76 and
color plate IV).
*David and Goliath* (plate 77).

DORIA GALLERY
*Rest during the Flight into Egypt*
(plates 15, 16).
*Mary Magdalen* (plate 17).
*St John the Baptist* (plate 18).

GALLERIA NAZIONALE D'ARTE
ANTICA
*Narcissus* (plate 19).
*St John the Baptist* (plate 52).

PINACOTECA VATICANA
*Burial of Christ* (plates 59, 60,
61).

ODESCALCHI BALBI COLLEC-
TION
*The Conversion of St Paul* (plates 33,
34).

CAPUCHIN CONVENT
*St Francis* (plate 54).

CHURCH OF SANT'AGOSTINO
*Madonna of the Pilgrims* (or *of
Loreto*) (plates 56, 57, 58).

CHURCH OF SAN LUIGI DEI
FRANCESI
*The Calling of St Matthew* (plates 24,
26, 27, 28).
*The Martyrdom of St Matthew*
(plates 25, 29, 30, 31).
*St Matthew and the Angel* (plate 32).

CHURCH OF SANTA MARIA
DEL POPOLO
*Crucifixion of St Peter* (plate 48).
*The Conversion of St Paul* (plates 48,
50, 51).

## SYRACUSE

CHURCH OF SANTA LUCIA
*Burial of St Lucy* (plates 91, 92).

## VALLETTA (MALTA)

CATHEDRAL OF ST JOHN THE
BAPTIST
*The Beheading of St John the Baptist*
(plate 88).
*St Jerome* (plate 89).

## VIENNA

KUNSTHISTORISCHES MUSEUM
*David and Goliath* (plate 72).
*Madonna of the Rosary* (plates 80, 81,
82).

## UNKNOWN OR TEM-
PORARY LOCATIONS

*The Cardsharps* (plates 11, 13).
*The Incredulity of St Thomas* (plate
53).
*St John the Baptist* (plate 55).

# SELECTED CRITICISM

The mark of this school is a single unbroken light shining from above without being reflected, as would happen in a room with one window and with walls painted black. In this way the light and shade are very bright and very dark and, consequently, give relief to the picture, but not in a natural way. This was not done or conceived in the manner of a previous century or older painters, like Raphael, Titian, Corregio, and others. In its method of working, this school is very observant of the truth, which it always keeps before its mind while working. . . .

G. MANCINI<br>
Ragguaglio, 1671.

He gave himself . . . to painting according to his own genius, and took no notice at all of the excellent statues of the ancients and Raphael's famous pictures, but scorned them. He set for himself nature alone as the object of his brush. Consequently, when he was shown the most famous statues of Phidias and Glycon so that he might make a study of them, he gave no other reply than to stretch out his hand towards the crowds of men and women, indicating that nature had provided him with sufficient masters. And, in order to add force and authority to his words, he called a gypsy women that happened to be passing in the street and took her to his lodging, where he drew her in the act of telling the future, as these women of the Egyptian race are accustomed to do. . . .

G. P. BELLORI<br>
Le vite, 1672.

Michelangelo Amerighi or Morigi from Caravaggio is memorable in this time, because he brought back painting from Mannerism to the truth, both in his forms, which he always drew from nature, and in the colors he used, which were always of rather soft vermilions and blues, and which he made up from a few genuine colors in the manner of Giorgione. Therefore, Annibale Caracci said in praise of him that he ground up flesh to make his colors.

L. LANZI
*Storia pittorica dell' Italia*, 1789.

Modern naturalism, in the strict sense, begins in its simplest form with Michelangelo da Caravaggio.     J. BURCKHARDT
*Der Cicerone*, 1866.

Against a colorism that had become a mannerism and a perpetual dramatic tension that had turned into rhetoric, Michelangelo da Caravaggio asserted the necessity of a contrast between light and shade that should be life, and a pose that should be reflection. Only after having made himself the complete master of reality and having discovered the strength of his own imagination did he begin to create the drama which, as is seen throughout all the new works which he had just completed, would no longer be rhetoric, but really drama.     L. VENTURI
*Il Caravaggio*, 1921.

. . . I know few works of art which like this one (*The Martyrdom of St Matthew*), so clearly and overwhelmingly affirm their stylistic intentions. The style is reduced, I could almost say, to something concrete and palpable. I remember few other figures in which the dynamism of the human body in its greatest tension is represented more simply than in the naked form of the executioner, where the highly original position of the shoulder, which dominates the whole body and becomes its "head" and key, makes the most effective and clearest possible impression of the act in a new and convincing manner. Note how Caravaggio once more saves himself from the "realistic" snare of chiaroscuro illusion by creating planes of light and darkness and doing away with the soft *penumbras*, and markings . . . sharp margins and crescents of light. . . .     M. MARANGONI
*Il Caravaggio*, 1922.

In Caravaggio, light surprises and fixes the form. . . . It shapes itself in concrete planes which penetrate into the picture and come from a source just a little way out of it, and move forward in only a few directions with the least angular variation.

In such conditions, if the movement of a gesture continued it would pass out of the shaft of light and return to the shade and vanish. The plastic masses stretch forward to reach the life-giving light. Where the light touched, there life is created; not swarming, diversified, and colored, but compact, savage, austere—violently scorning all that is contingent, transitory, and decorative.          L. DAMI in OJETTI-DAMI-TARCHIANI, *La pittura italiana del Seicento e del Settecento*, 1924.

From his predecessors' experience of light (amongst whom were Lotto, whom Lomazzo . . . calls "master of the art of painting light" and Savoldo, whose "ingenious description of darkness" was praised by Pino), Caravaggio discovered the "form of shadows," a style where light is no longer enslaved to the plastic definition of the bodies upon which it falls, but instead, together with the accompanying shadow, is master of their very existence. For the first time the principle of the element was immaterial, a question now not of a body but of substance, an essence external to and surrounding man, and not his slave. . . . It was easy to see the meaning of this style in comparison with the Renaissance, which had started from man, and had built up a superb anthropocentric edifice, for which light was only a sub-ordinate adornment. In the place of artifice and dramatic stylistic symbolism, light itself now appeared, not just an idea of it. But when a thing was caught in a flash of light there was no longer any chance of deciding beforehand what its form should be, nor the design, nor its style, nor even the rarity of its color, and so the object came out in stark naturalness. The breaking up of the darkness revealed what had happened and only what had happened, whence the inexorable naturalness and inescapable variety,

the inability "to choose." Men, objects, forms, all were on the same plane, sharing in the same style of existence and not subject to an imposed scale of values. . . .                    R. LONGHI
*Quesiti caravaggeschi*, 1928–9

No typical form of the Baroque is to be found in Caravaggio. His development in profundity and clarity put him beside the artists of the Quattrocento, rather than those of his own time. In him there is an epic humanity, and an apostolic intention very different from the Baroque spirit. His meditative style has been deepened and concentrated in a single direction and places him in historical solitude in the era of the Baroque and carries him beyond it.                              C. L. RAGGHIANTI
*Cultura artistica e arte barocca*, 1933

This work [*The Conversion of St Paul*, plate 49] is one of the first and greatest milestones in the course of modern painting; not so much for its powerful "reality" as for its new and revolutionary language and style. In fact, Caravaggio is the painter who first looks at life with eyes that have been freed from the blindfold of every official, cultural, and intellectual tradition. Not even Titian was so immune. This horse has been "seen" for the first time as it really was and with a "democratic" eye and spirit, as free as that of nineteenth-century impressionist's. . . .

M. MARANGONI
*Come si guarda un quadro*, 1948

# BIBLIOGRAPHICAL NOTE

G. BAGLIONE. *Le vite de' pittori, scultori ed architetti dal pontificato di Gregorio VIII del 1572 fino a' tempi di Papa Urbano VIII nel 1642*, Rome, 1642.

G. MANCINI. *Ragguaglio della vita di alcuni pittori*, codice Marciano (1671), edited by L. Venturi, in *L'Arte*, 1910.

G. P. BELLORI. *Le vite de' pittori, scultori ed architetti moderni*, Rome, 1672.

W. KALLAB. "Caravaggio" in *Jahrbuch der Kunsthistorischen Sammlungen der allerhöchsten Kaiserhauses*, 1906–7.

L. VENTURI. "Studi su Michelangelo da Caravaggio," in *L'Arte*, 1910.

G. ROUCHÈS. *Le Caravage*, Paris, 1920.

L. VENTURI. *Il Caravaggio*, Florence, 1922.

H. VOSS. *Die Malerei des Barock* in *Rom*, Berlin, 1924.

E. BENKARD. *Caravaggio Studien*, Berlin, 1928.

L. ZAHN. *Caravaggio*, Berlin, 1928.

R. LONGHI. "Quesiti caravaggeschi," in *Pinacotheca*, 1928–9.

L. SCHUDT. *Caravaggio*, Vienna, 1942.

R. LONGHI. "Ultimi studi sul Caravaggio e la sua cerchia," in *Proporzioni*, 1943.

B. BERENSON. *Del Caravaggio, delle sue incongruenze e della sua fama*, Florence, 1951.

*Exhibition of Caravaggio and his followers*, Milan, in the Royal Palace, 1951. Catalogue, Florence, 1951.

J. HESS. "The Chronology of the Contarelli Chapel," in *The Burlington Magazine*, June, 1951.

D. MAHON. *Caravaggio revised*, July, 1951.

R. LONGHI. "Il Caravaggio e i suoi dipinti a San Luigi dei Francesi; La Giuditta nel percorso del Caravaggio," and other studies in *Paragone*, 1951, nn. 17, 19, 21.

L. VENTURI. *Caravaggio*, Novara, 1951.

D. MAHON. "An addition to Caravaggio's early period," in *Paragone*, 1952, n. 25.

R. LONGHI. "'L'Ecce Homo' del Caravaggio a Genova," in *Paragone*, 1954, n. 51.

# REPRODUCTIONS

## ACKNOWLEDGEMENT FOR REPRODUCTIONS

Plate 11, *Braun*; plate 12, *Hanfstangl*; plate 18, *Alinari*; plates 59–61 and 65–8, *Anderson*; plates 6–7 and 36–7, *Superintendent of the Florence Galleries*; color plates I–IV, *Scala*.

The following are reproduced by courtesy of the respective museums: plates 9, 20, 22, 23, 41–6, 53, 62, 63, 80–2, 88 and 89.

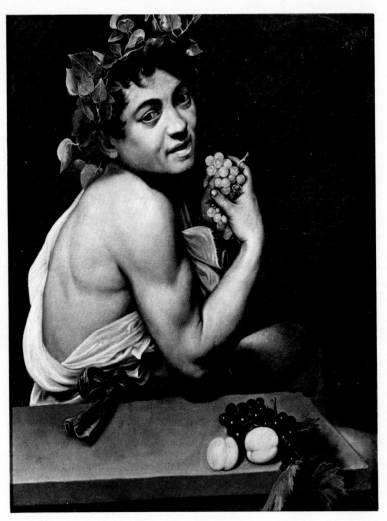

THE SICK BACCHUS,
Rome, Borghese Gallery

Plate 1. BOY WITH A BASKET OF FRUIT,
Rome, Borghese Gallery

Plate 2. THE SICK BACCHUS,
Rome, Borghese Gallery

Plate 3. BOY BITTEN BY A LIZARD,
Florence, Roberto Longhi Collection

Plate 4. *Detail of plate 3*

Plate 5. BACCHUS,
Florence, Uffizi

Plate 6. *Detail of plate 5*

Plate 7. *Detail of plate 5*

Plate 8. THE LUTE PLAYER,
Leningrad, Hermitage

Plate 9. THE CONCERT,
New York, Metropolitan Museum of Art

Plate 10. THE FORTUNE TELLER,
Paris, Louvre

Plate II. THE CARDSHARPS,
location unknown

Plate 12. *Detail of plate 10*

Plate 13. *Detail of plate 11*

Plate 14. ECSTASY OF ST FRANCIS,
Hartford (Mass.), Wadsworth Atheneum

Plate 15. REST DURING THE FLIGHT INTO EGYPT,
Rome, Doria Gallery

Plate 16. *Detail of plate 15*

MEDUSA,
Florence, Uffizi

Plate 17. MARY MAGDALEN,
Rome, Doria Gallery

Plate 18. ST JOHN THE BAPTIST,
Rome, Doria Gallery

Plate 19. NARCISSUS,
Rome, Galleria Nazionale

Plate 20. PORTRAIT OF A WOMAN,
now destroyed

Plate 21. ST CATHERINE,
Lugano, Schloss Rohoncz Foundation

Plate 22. ST MATTHEW AND THE ANGEL,
now destroyed

Plate 23. *Detail of plate 22*

Plate 24. THE CALLING OF ST MATTHEW,
Rome, Church of San Luigi dei Francesi

Plate 25. THE MARTYRDOM OF ST MATTHEW,
Rome, Church of San Luigi dei Francesi

Plate 26. *Detail of plate 24*

Plate 27. *Detail of plate 24*

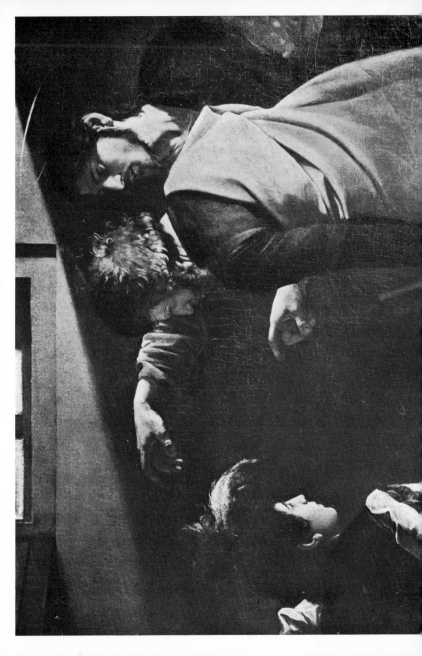

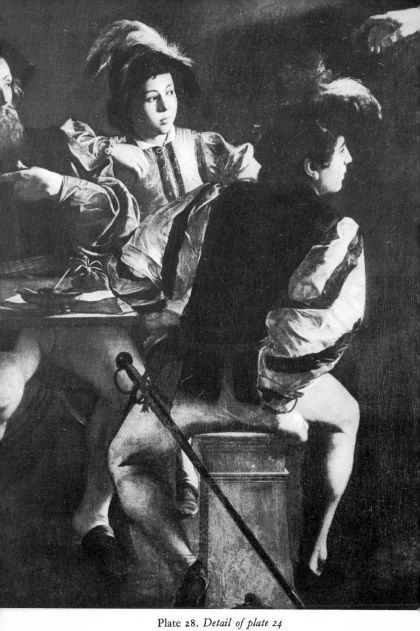

Plate 28. *Detail of plate 24*

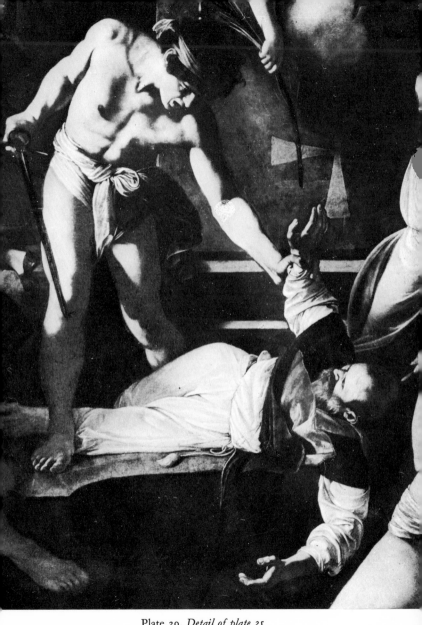

Plate 29. *Detail of plate 25*

Plate 30. *Detail of plate 25*

Plate 31. *Detail of plate 25*

Plate 32. ST MATTHEW AND THE ANGEL,
Rome, Church of San Luigi dei Francesi

Plate 33. THE CONVERSION OF ST PAUL,
Rome, Odescalchi Balbi Collection

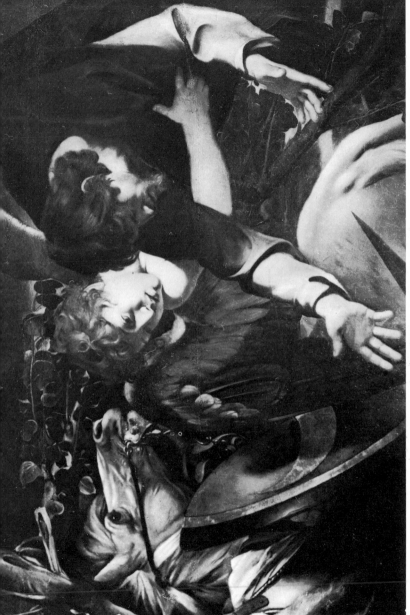

Plate 24. Detail of plate 23

Plate 35. THE SACRIFICE OF ISAAC,
Florence, Uffizi

Plate 36. *Detail of plate 35*

Plate 37. *Detail of plate 35*

Plate 39. *Detail of plate 38*

Plate 40. MEDUSA,
Florence, Uffizi

Plate 41. THE SUPPER AT EMMAUS,
London, National Gallery

Plate 42. *Detail of plate 41*

Plate 43. *Detail of plate 41*

Plate 44. *Detail of plate 41*

Plate 45. *Detail of plate 41*

Plate 46. *Detail of plate 41*

Plate 47. BASKET OF FRUIT,
Milan, Pinacoteca Ambrosiana

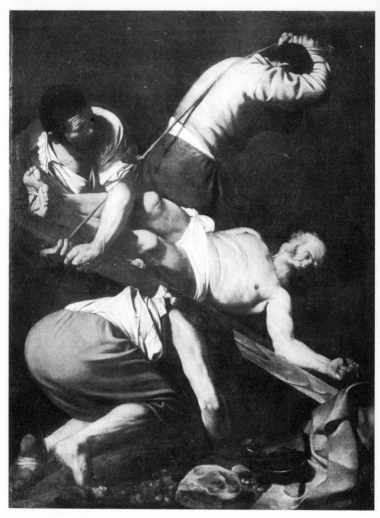

Plate 48. THE CRUCIFIXION OF ST PETER,
Rome, Church of Santa Maria del Popolo, Cerasi Chapel

Plate 49. THE CONVERSION OF ST PAUL,
Rome, Church of Santa Maria del Popolo, Cerasi Chapel

Plate 50. *Detail of plate 49*

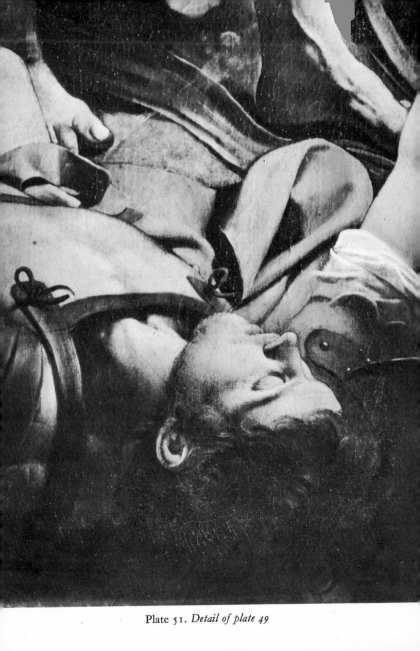

Plate 51. *Detail of plate 49*

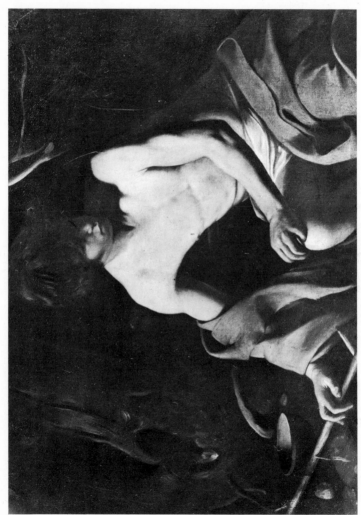

Plate 52. ST JOHN THE BAPTIST,
Rome, Galleria Nazionale d'Arte Antica

Plate 53: THE INCREDULITY OF ST THOMAS,
now lost

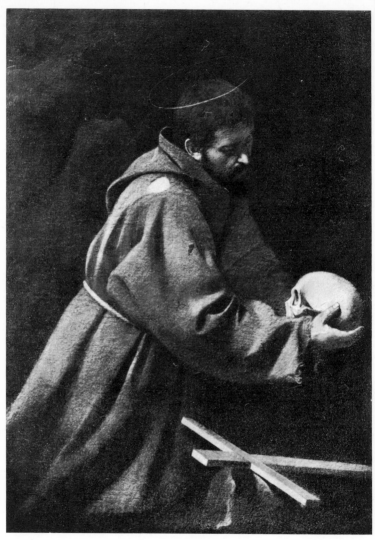

Plate 54. ST FRANCIS,
Rome, Capuchin Convent

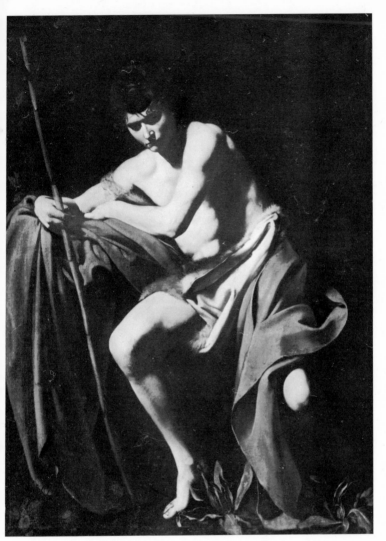

Plate 55. ST JOHN THE BAPTIST,
Great Britain, Private Collection

Plate 56. MADONNA OF THE PILGRIMS,
Rome, Church of Sant'Agostino

Plate 57. *Detail of plate 56*

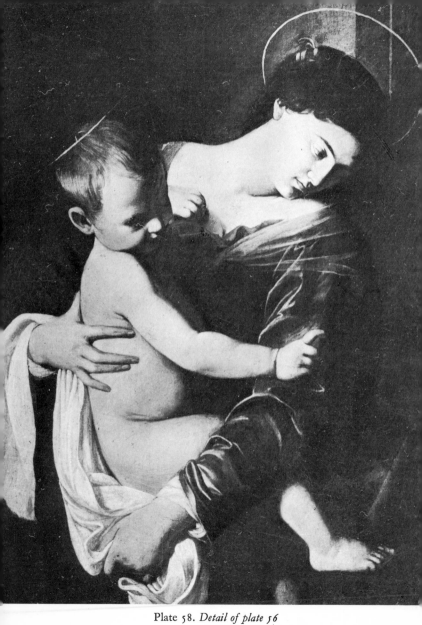

Plate 58. *Detail of plate 56*

Plate 59. BURIAL OF CHRIST,
Rome, Pinocoteca Vaticana

Plate 60. *Detail of plate 59*

ST JEROME,
Rome, Borghese Gallery

Plate 61. *Detail of plate 59*

Plate 62. CHRIST ON THE MOUNT OF OLIVES,
now destroyed

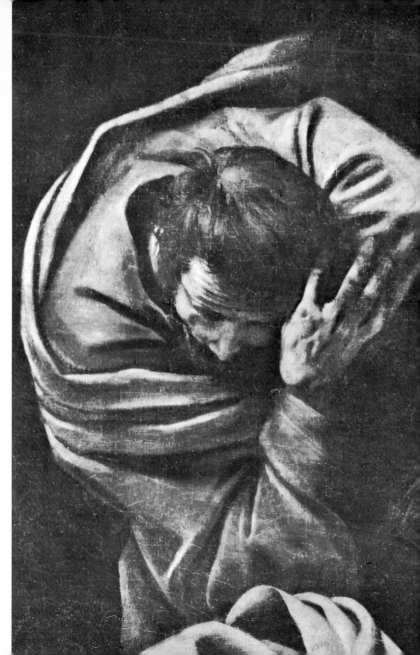

Plate 64. MADONNA OF THE PALAFRENIERI,
Rome, Borghese Gallery

Plate 65. DEATH OF THE VIRGIN,
Paris, Louvre

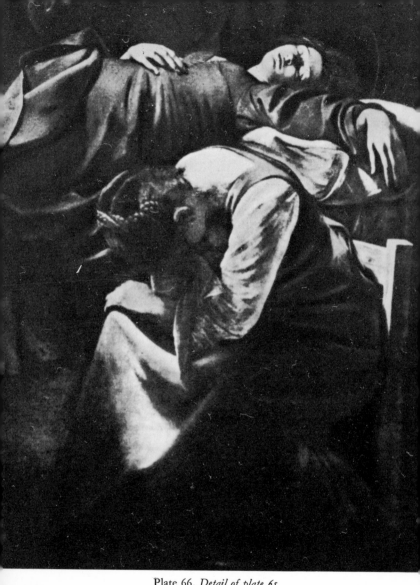

Plate 66. *Detail of plate 65*

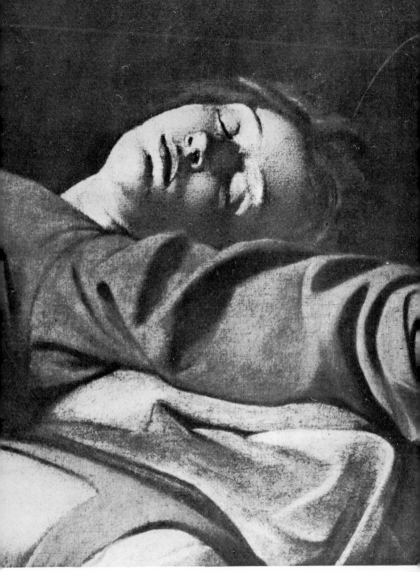

Plate 67. *Detail of plate 65*

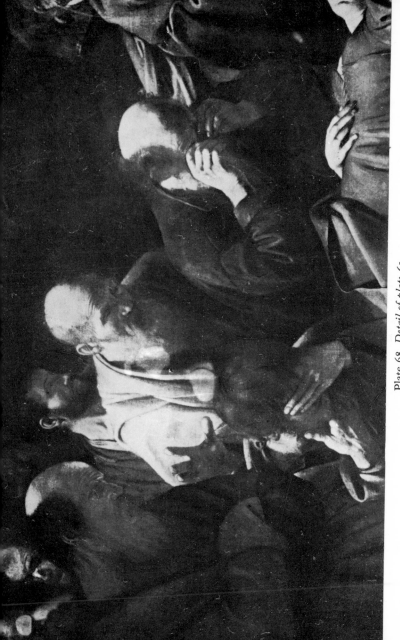

Plate 68. *Detail of plate 65*

Plate 69. THE SUPPER AT EMMAUS,
Milan, Brera

Plate 70. *Detail of plate 69*

Plate 71. *Detail of plate 69*

Plate 72. DAVID AND GOLIATH,
Vienna, Kunsthistorisches Museum

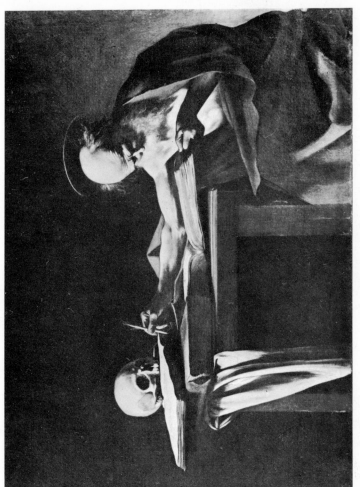

Plate 73. ST JEROME,
Rome, Borghese Gallery

Plate 74. *Detail of plate 73*

Plate 75. ST JEROME,
Barcelona, Montserrat Monastery

Plate 76. ST JOHN THE BAPTIST,
Rome, Borghese Gallery

ST JOHN THE BAPTIST,
Rome, Borghese Gallery

Plate 77. DAVID AND GOLIATH,
Rome, Borghese Gallery

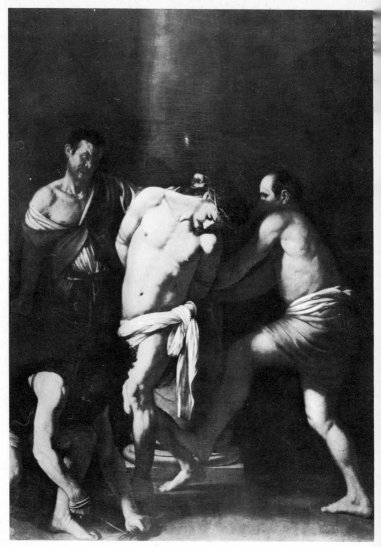

Plate 78. THE SCOURGING OF CHRIST,
Naples, Church of San Domenico Maggiore

Plate 79. *Detail of plate 78*

Plate 80. MADONNA OF THE ROSARY,
Vienna, Kunsthistorisches Museum

Plate 81. *Detail of plate 80*

Plate 82. *Detail of plate 80*

Plate 83. SALOME WITH THE HEAD OF JOHN THE BAPTIST,
Madrid, The Escorial

Plate 84. THE SEVEN WORKS OF MERCY,
Naples, Pio Monte della Misericordia

Plate 85. *Detail of plate 84*

Plate 86. *Detail of plate 84*

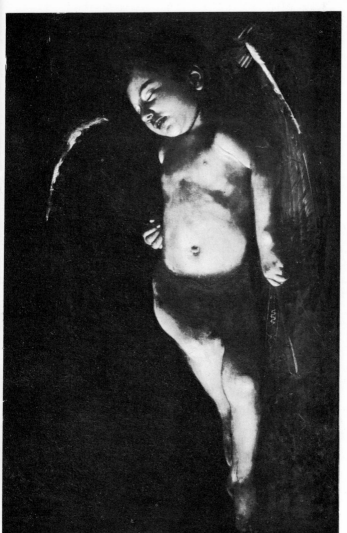

Plate 87. SLEEPING CUPID,
Florence, Pitti Palace

Plate 88. BEHEADING OF JOHN THE BAPTIST,
Valletta, Cathedral of St John the Baptist

Plate 89, ST JEROME,
Valletta, Cathedral of St John the Baptist

Plate 90. ALOF DE WIGNACOURT,
Paris, Louvre

Plate 91. BURIAL OF ST LUCY,
Syracuse, Church of Santa Lucia

Plate 92. *Detail of plate 91*

Plate 93. THE RAISING OF LAZARUS,
Messina, Museo Nazionale

Plate 94. ADORATION OF THE SHEPHERDS,
Messina, Museo Nazionale

Plate 95. *Detail of plate 94*

Plate 96. NATIVITY WITH SS LAURENCE AND FRANCIS,
Palermo, Oratory of San Lorenzo